Contents

I0887648

About the Author

Ian Baxter is a military historian who specialises in German twentieth century military history. He has written more than fifty books including *Poland – The Eighteen Day Victory March*, *Panzers In North Africa*, *The Ardennes Offensive*, *The Western Campaign*, *The 12th SS Panzer-Division Hitlerjugend*, *The Waffen-SS on the Western Front*, *The Waffen-SS on the Eastern Front*, *The Red Army at Stalingrad*, *Elite German Forces of World War II*, *Armoured Warfare*, *German Tanks of War*, *Blitzkrieg*, *Panzer-Divisions at War*, *Hitler's Panzers*, *German Armoured Vehicles of World War Two*, *Last Two Years of the Waffen-SS at War*, *German Soldier Uniforms and Insignia*, *German Guns of the Third Reich*, *Defeat to Retreat: The Last Years of the German Army At War 1943–45*, *Operation Bagration – the Destruction of Army Group Centre*, *German Guns of the Third Reich*, *Rommel and the Afrika Korps*, *U-Boat War*, and most recently *The Sixth Army and the Road to Stalingrad*. He has written over a hundred articles including 'Last days of Hitler', 'Wolf's Lair', 'The Story of the V1 and V2 Rocket Programme', 'Secret Aircraft of World War Two', 'Rommel at Tobruk', 'Hitler's War With his Generals', 'Secret British Plans to Assassinate Hitler', 'The SS at Arnhem', 'Hitlerjugend', 'Battle of Caen 1944', 'Gebirgsjäger at War', 'Panzer Crews', 'Hitlerjugend Guerrillas', 'Last Battles in the East', 'The Battle of Berlin', and many more. He has also reviewed numerous military studies for publication, supplied thousands of photographs and important documents to various publishers and film production companies worldwide, and lectures to various schools, colleges and universities throughout the United Kingdom and the Republic of Ireland.

Introduction

Preparing for war

Following the invasion of Poland in October 1939, Reichsführer-SS Heinrich Himmler, commander of the SS, was eager to expand the Waffen-SS and wanted to establish a number of new SS divisions and recruit thousands of new soldiers under his command. This included recruiting ethnic Germans from occupied territories. As these were not technically eligible for conscription, he knew that the Wehrmacht could not obstruct his plans. Thus he began a recruitment drive which would be much better, more organised and larger than ever before. Apart from the expansion of the Leibstandarte, the three SS-Verfügungstruppe Standarten – Deutschland, Germania and Der Führer, which later became Das Reich, Totenkopf, and Polizei – Himmler was also enthusiastic to recruit foreign blood for what he termed a 'crusade against Bolshevism'. Conscription for foreign recruits began in April 1940 with the establishment of two regiments: the Waffen-SS Regiment Westland (for Dutch and Flemish volunteers) and a Waffen-SS Regiment Nordland (for Danish, Norwegian, and Swedish volunteers).

Himmler wanted an international army which would attract 'all the Nordic blood of the world' in one single crusade which would represent the spirit of a New Europe, all aimed at the destruction of 'godless Bolshevism'. Thus a new Nordic formation was constructed at the behest of the Reichsführer. It was originally organised as the Nordische Division (Nr. 5), and its core of men was composed of eager Nordic volunteers and ethnic German Waffen-SS personnel. In late 1940 the SS Infantry Regiment Germania of the SS-Verfügungs-Division, which had drafted mainly ethnic Germans into its units, was incorporated into its formation to bolster the newly recreated division. In December 1940, the new SS division was to be designated as SS-Division Germania. However, in early 1941, its name was changed to SS-Division Wiking. The Wiking division comprised of three motorised infantry regiments: Nordland, Westland, and Germania. In addition to its infantry regiments, an artillery regiment was added: SS Artillery Regiment 5.

Chosen to command this division was Brigadeführer Felix Steiner. Steiner had been introduced to Himmler in mid-1940 and had formerly been the commander of the Verfügungstruppe SS Regiment Deutschland. He was soon nominated by the Reichsführer to oversee the creation of, and then take command of, the new Wiking Division, which comprised mainly non-German volunteers, mostly Dutch, Flemish, Finns and Scandinavians, and included the Danish regiment Frikorps Danmark.

This was the first multi-national division in the German army and would not be the last. In fact, two years later four of the eight new SS divisions formed would comprise foreign conscripts, mainly eastern Europeans.

Himmler was determined that Wiking be prepared for the war against Russia and be indoctrinated to fight against Bolshevism. He looked upon the fight against the Soviet Union as a righteous crusade with the SS order taking the glory on the battlefield. His plans were intoxicated by his personal over-optimistic ambitions and dreams of destroying Russia and colonizing it. The planning for the invasion of Russia was far different from the Reichsführer's vision. From the onset of planning, little was known about the country they were about to attack. The Red Army were an enigma to the German soldier. There was little information supplied about the country which they were invading, nor was there anything substantial known about the terrain or climate. The SS saw the Russians as inferior Slavic people. Propaganda informed the German soldier that all Russians were living in poverty and that its antiquated army were totally unprepared for war. They therefore seriously underestimated their enemy and were unprepared for the unimaginable distances in which they had to march. The immense forests, the huge expanses of marshland, and the many rivers that were continuously prone to flooding would be huge obstacles in their march east. The little information they did have was often incorrect. Maps frequently showed none of the roads, and the roads that were on the maps were in a terrible state of repair or nothing more than dirt tracks.

There were also extremes of temperature in Russia: tropical mosquito-infested swamplands in the north; baking open arid terrain in the south; in the autumn the rain would turn roads and tracks into slurry; in winter temperatures could drop to thirty or even forty degrees below and Russia would freeze for weeks on end.

Despite these hardships, the men of Wiking were determined to fulfill their duty and undertake their war of annihilation against the Soviet Union.

(**Opposite, above**) Fresh-faced newly recruited soldiers of the SS Wiking Division with their motorcycles at a training camp. The men of the division were recruited from foreign volunteers in Denmark, Norway, Sweden, Finland, Estonia, the Netherlands and Belgium under the command of German officers. The division was formed in December 1940 around the Germania regiment from the SS Division Verfügungstruppe, which later became Das Reich. The division was initially titled Germania, but in January 1941 the name changed to Wiking to reflect the Nordic non-German volunteers that had been recruited. The division comprised SS Infantry Regiment Nordland which was composed of Danes and Norwegians, SS Infantry Regiment Westland of Dutch and Flemish, and Infantry Regiment Germania comprising the 5th SS Artillery Regiment which was made up entirely of ethnic Germans.

(**Opposite, below**) Wiking soldiers in the Spring of 1941 stand next to a light Horch cross-country vehicle and a supply truck inside a village. Local children can be seen with the troops. Note the divisional markings of SS Wiking painted in white on the right front fender of both vehicles.

IMAGES OF WAR

5th SS WIKING AT WAR 1941-1945

A HISTORY OF THE DIVISION

RARE PHOTOGRAPHS FROM WARTIME ARCHIVES

Ian Baxter

Pen & Sword
MILITARY

First published in Great Britain in 2018 by
PEN & SWORD MILITARY
An imprint of
Pen & Sword Books Ltd
47 Church Street
Barnsley
South Yorkshire
S70 2AS

ISBN 978-1-52672-134-1

A CIP catalogue record for this book is available from the British Library.

Typeset by Concept, Huddersfield, West Yorkshire HD4 5JL.
Printed and bound in England by CPI Group (UK) Ltd, Croydon CR0 4YY.

Pen & Sword Books Limited incorporates the imprints of Atlas, Archaeology, Aviation, Discovery, Family History, Fiction, History, Maritime, Military, Military Classics, Politics, Select, Transport, True Crime, Air World, Frontline Publishing, Leo Cooper, Remember When, Seaforth Publishing, The Praetorian Press, Wharncliffe Local History, Wharncliffe Transport, Wharncliffe True Crime and White Owl.

For a complete list of Pen & Sword titles please contact
PEN & SWORD BOOKS LIMITED
47 Church Street, Barnsley, South Yorkshire S70 2AS, England
E-mail: enquiries@pen-and-sword.co.uk
Website: www.pen-and-sword.co.uk

STANDARD

During a training exercise and men of SS Wiking can be seen in a field. Note that they are all wearing the SS M40 Feldmütze 'Schiffchen' (enlisted man's overseas cap) which was worn throughout the war by the division.

Commanding officers confer during a training exercise in the spring of 1941. During this period the division was training for operations in southern Russia. The division saw extensive training in Heuberg in Germany and was deemed ready for combat by April 1941. A few weeks later in May it was given orders to be transported through Poland to prepare for action against the Soviet Union.

Two photographs taken in the same area in southern Poland in the spring of 1941 showing a column of support vehicles. They have the 'Wiking' divisional insignia painted on the front right fender. Only weeks later the division would be ordered to move across the Polish border in Galicia near Tarnapol and attack Russia.

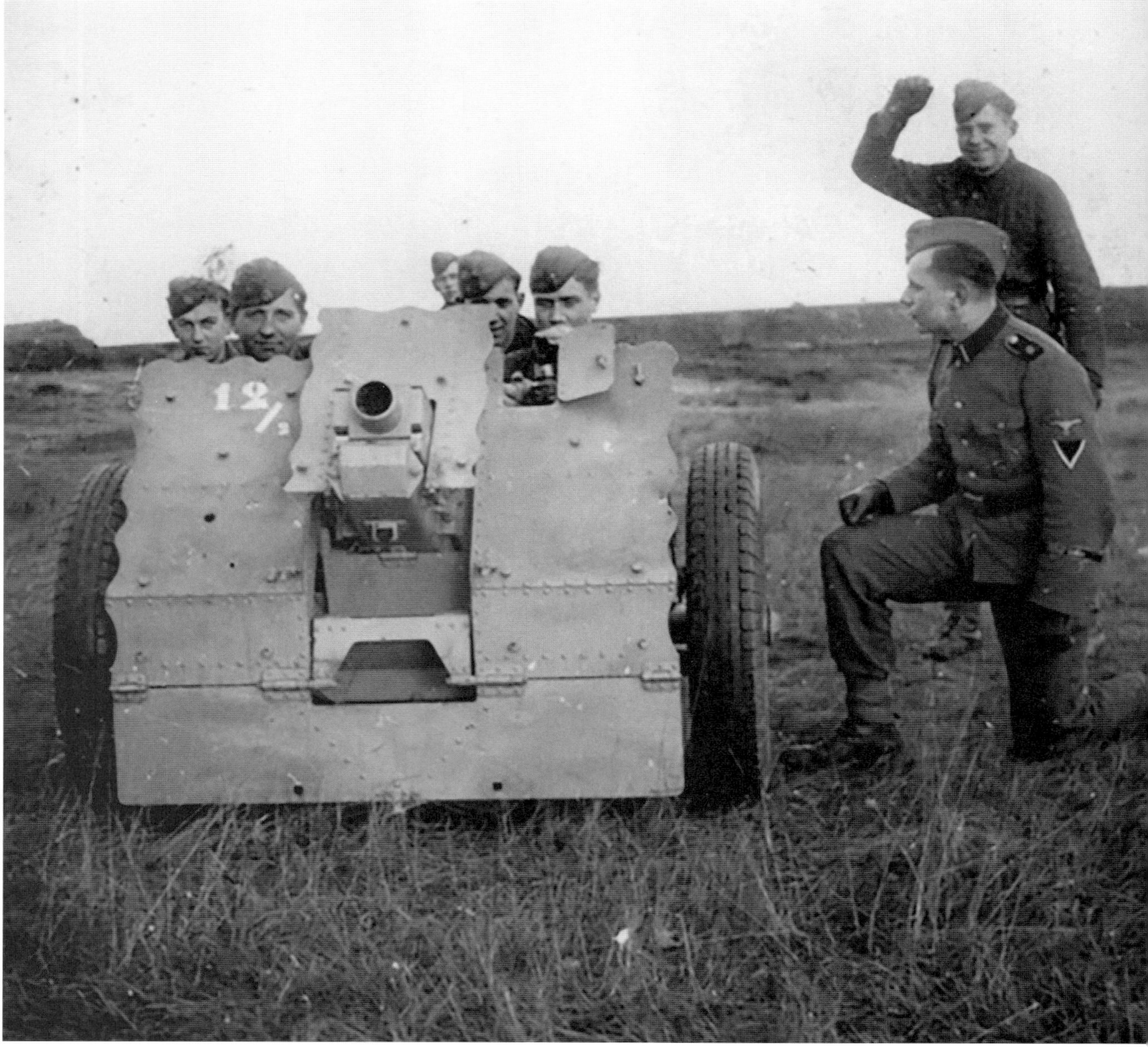

During training and a PaK crew pose for the camera behind the gun shield of their 7.5cm le.IG18 gun. This weapon was one of the first post-First World War guns to be issued to the regular army and later to the Waffen-SS. It was light and robust and employed a shotgun breech action. A typical infantry regiment controlled three infantry battalions, an infantry gun company with six 7.5cm le.IG18 and two 15cm s.IG33 guns, and an anti-tank company with twelve 3.7cm PaK35/36 guns.

Cuff title of SS Wiking. Members of the division were issued with cuff bands bearing the unit title Wiking. The cuff band was machine-embroidered Latin script with Wiking stitched in silver and grey cotton thread on black rayon.

Chapter One

Baptism of Fire in the East

The 5th SS Division Wiking was sent to Heuberg in Germany for training and was deemed ready for combat by April 1941. A few weeks later in May it was given orders to be transported through Poland to prepare for action against the Soviet Union. It was to take part in Army Group South's advance into the Ukraine under the command of General von Rundstedt. In Army Group South it comprised six infantry divisions with some 600 tanks distributed among them which were to bulldoze their way through thinly-held Russian defences.

On the morning of 22 June 1941 the German army, comprising some 3 million troops, attacked a bewildered Russian force along an 1,800-mile front. The main thrust in the south was directed between the southern edge of the Pripet Marshes and the foothills of the Carpathian Mountains. Here Rundstedt concentrated the whole of the 1st Panzer Army, 6th Army and 17th Army. The 6th Army was under the faithful command of Field Marshal von Reichenau and consisted of three Army Corps and one reserve. Reichenau had commanded the 6th Army during the battle of France in 1940, but the army had already made a name for itself during the invasion of Poland. Wiking was held back in reserve during the initial stages of the Russian invasion and was not released until 29 June when it was ordered through Galicia near Tarnapol.

Near the city the division forced a crossing of the River Slucz and, with other Waffen-SS units, soon engaged in heavy fighting. It did not take long before this fresh new SS division overwhelmed the enemy, despite being harassed by strong Russian forces that had been cut off in the wooded swampland between the Pripet Marshes and the Carpathians. As Wiking pushed on towards the Dnieper River its primary task was to hold onto as much ground as possible and prevent enemy formations from retreating intact into Russia.

Over the days and weeks that followed, Wiking and other divisions within Army Group South accelerated. Again and again the Russians were overwhelmed by the German onslaught. By August the 6th Army had swung out east of Kiev as German forces began mopping up the last remnants in and around the besieged city. When the battle of Kiev finally ended on 21 September 1941 almost 665,000 Russian troops had been captured in the encirclement. Exhilarated by the fall of Kiev the German army mercilessly pushed forward leaving behind it a trail of destruction. Across

Reichenau's front tanks and troops hammered deeper, and the guns of the infantry divisions lengthened their range. It seemed that Blitzkrieg had once again been imprinted on the battlefield and the men felt invincible.

During August 1941 the Wiking Division continued its advance and established a defensive perimeter around a bridgehead across the Dnieper River. Despite determined attacks by strong Russian forces the division held its line and then advanced towards Rostov-on-Don. It then took part in the battle for Rostov.

The battles in and around Rostov became a fierce contest of attrition, and although the Russians showed great fortitude and determination, they were constantly hampered by lack of weapons and manpower needed to sustain them on the battlefield. The remaining troops holding out in the city were subjected to merciless ground and aerial bombardments. The situation for the defenders looked grim. The German attack was without respite. Russian commanders insisted that their troops must fight from fixed positions without any tactical retreat and hold on to the death. Consequently, stiff resistance began to hinder German progress and losses in men and equipment mounted. As the situation deteriorated, Rundstedt, against Hitler's orders, ordered Kleist's 1st Panzer Army, which included Division Wiking, to evacuate Rostov and fall back over the Mius River, some 60 miles west of the city.

On the night of 30 November Rundstedt was relieved of his command and replaced by Reichenau. However Reichenau himself agreed with Rundstedt's plan to evacuate Rostov. It was the first significant German withdrawal of the war. A few days later a 43-year-old staff officer called Friedrich Wilhelm Ernst Paulus was promoted to command the 6th Army. It was hoped that Paulus could win the winter war of 1941. However, not even Paulus's determination could prevent Army Group South from becoming stagnated across the freezing plains of the Soviet Union. When the snow settled and temperatures dropped, many soldiers were reluctant to emerge from their shelters to fight. Hundreds of tanks and other vehicles were abandoned in the drifting snow and despair gripped Army Group South.

Reichenau's policy to withdraw 1st Panzer Army from Rostov with the Wiking Division and hold his battered frost-bitten forces behind the Mius had saved ground, but at an alarming expenditure in men and material. The Russians, as predicted, had finally run out of power because of the harsh weather, and were unable to achieve any deep penetration into the German lines. This had saved Army Group South from serious loss.

Reichenau had failed to capture Rostov, and his forces stood along a river line crucified by the Russian winter and fanatical Soviet resistance. As for Wiking, the division licked its wounds and recouped its strength behind the Mius. Some had said the division was not battle ready and been simply thrown into the line to bolster numbers, but they had fought well. As the New Year of 1942 opened, Wiking would show its worth once again, earning the respect it had deserved on the battlefield.

When the German army attacked the Soviet Union in the early hours of 22 June 1941, Wiking was held back in reserve and was not released until 29 June when it was ordered through Galicia near Tarnapol. Near to the city the division then forced a crossing of the River Slucz and, with other Waffen-SS units, soon engaged in heavy fighting. Here in this photograph a Wiking soldier watches a Russian tank burn after it has been hit by anti-tank fire.

Wiking troops wearing their distinctive SS summer camouflage smocks inside a wooded area during the early phase of operations in Russia in the summer of 1941. They are all wearing the M40 field cap and their M35 steel helmets are attached to their black leather infantryman belts.

Wiking mortar crew wearing their summer camouflage smocks in action. The crew are using an 8cm Granatwerfer 34 (8cm GrW 34) which was the standard German infantry mortar throughout the war. It was common for infantry, especially during intensive long periods of action, to fire their mortar from either trenches or dug-in positions where the crew could be protected from enemy fire.

(**Opposite, above**) The initial stages of the war in Russia went well for Wiking and many Red Army troops were captured. In this photograph a motorcyclist follows a column of dejected Russian PoWs to a fate that can only be imagined.

(**Opposite, below**) A column of prime movers, more than likely part of a battery, hauling 15cm field howitzers towards the battle front along a dusty road. This gun was used extensively on the Eastern Front and primarily designed to attack targets deeper in the enemy's rear. These included command posts, reserve units, assembly areas, and logistics facilities.

(**Above**) A photograph showing Russian soldiers taken prisoner in the Rostov area in August 1941.

Two photographs showing Russian soldiers and Russian female personnel taken prisoner in the Rostov area in August 1941. During August the Wiking division had established a defensive perimeter around a bridgehead across the Dnieper River. Despite determined attacks by strong Russian forces the division held the line and then advanced towards Rostov-on-Don. It then took part in the battle for Rostov capturing many Russian soldiers.

A heavy machine gun troop with their 7.92cm MG34 on a tripod mount during a fire mission. A heavy machine gun troop was provided with a tripod mount (Lafette 34) with a pair of leather carrying slings (Trageriemen), a long-range optical sight (Zieleinrichtung 34), at least one spare double-barrel carrier (Laufbehalter 34), a belt filling device (Gurtfuller 34), a number of 300-round metal cartridge cases, plus various items of cleaning equipment. The gunner can be seen looking through the long-range optical sight while his No. 2 is feeding the bullets.

A Wiking soldier, armed with a Karabiner 98K bolt action rifle with fixed bayonet, escorts Russian PoWs to the rear. One of the Red Army soldiers is injured and is being helped by two of his comrades.

Two Wiking soldiers in full battle dress during summer operations in 1941. The soldier on the left, who is probably a unit leader, is armed with the 9mm MP38/40 machine pistol, one of the most effective sub-machine guns ever produced. He is also wearing the MP38/40 magazine pouch, M1939 infantry support straps and an entrenching tool. The other soldier also has an entrenching tool which can be seen supported inside his black leather infantryman's belt. He is also wearing 6 × 30 field binoculars. Note the foliage attached to their M35 steel helmets secured by a rubber ring. Foliage can also be seen attached to the infantry support straps.

Wiking troops during operations on the Eastern Front in the summer of 1941. All three men are wearing their summer camouflage smocks with their 6 x 30 field binoculars, and appear to be ranked squad leaders or SS-Rottenführer.

Red Army soldiers have surrendered to a Wiking unit. During the summer of 1941 the Wiking division enjoyed a series of successful engagements against their bewildered foe. Not only did the initial German attack against the Red Army catch them in a state of unpreparedness, but also many of the Russians lacked war experience compared to the Germans. Also the old border fortifications along the Soviet frontier were still incomplete, and as a result the Russians were unable to hold a line of resistance.

A motorcycle combination unit advancing along a sandy road wearing their distinctive summer camouflage smocks. The motorcycle was used for both combat and reconnaissance roles. Each infantry and Panzer division incorporated hundreds of motorcycles which were distributed among the Panzer and rifle regiments, Flak detachments, artillery regiments, supply units, signals and reconnaissance units. One of the hazards of travelling by motorcycle, especially in the Soviet Union, was the lack of good-quality roads for vehicles. Motorcyclists sometimes decided to avoid the roads and travel across country, which often proved perilous. The casualty rate among motorcyclists was high.

A 15cm s.FH18 battery being prepared for a fire mission. This weapon was the standard artillery piece in a division. Both infantry and motorized artillery regiments became the backbone of the fighting in the early years on the Russian front. Wicker ammunition cases stacked at a distance from the gun and primed shells lying near the artillery pieces.

A group of Wiking soldiers pause in their advance wearing their distinctive Waffen-SS battle dress and full gear. Among the riflemen are heavy MG34 machine gunners carrying ammunition and the folded Lafette 34 tripod mount.

The first of two photographs taken in sequence showing what appears to be a Wiking unit during a reconnaissance mission advancing through a river.

The second photograph shows an SS-Sturmführer negotiating the river bank; he appears to be armed with an MP38/40 machine gun.

A photograph showing a battery of 15cm heavy field howitzers during a fire mission , one before going into action, the other during a fire mission near the Dnieper River. It was here that Wiking was given its primary task to hold onto as much ground as possible and prevent retreating enemy formations from withdrawing into Russia.

Two photographs showing destroyed Russian armour and vehicles during Wiking's advance through southern Russia in the summer of 1941 in the Kiev region.

Two photographs taken in sequence showing a captured Russian bunker near Kiev in the summer of 1941. A Wiking Flak gunner can be seen with his 2cm Flak gun. When the battle of Kiev ended on 21 September 1941, some 665,000 Russian troops were captured in the encirclement. Exhilarated by the fall of Kiev the German Army mercilessly pushed forward leaving a trail of devastation in its wake.

A prime mover towing a 15cm howitzer towards the battlefront in 1941.

Two Sd.Kfz.10/4 halftracks, mounting the 2cm Flak gun, have pulled up inside a wooded area with a Wiking unit. Various support vehicles too have parked in the wooded clearing, more than likely to rest and resupply before resuming their drive.

An MG34 machine gun set up on an anti-aircraft tripod with two Wiking machine gunners. The weapon has the MG34 50-round basket drum magazine attached. The ammunition box, concealed, will have been placed beneath the weapon for easy access. These soldiers are probably attached to an artillery battery. Artillery batteries were provided with two 7.92mm light machine guns for self defence both from ground and aerial attack.

A close-up posed shot of a Wiking infantryman armed with a Karabiner 98K rifle with rifle site. He is wearing a summer camouflage smock, and aviator goggles are seen on his M35 steel helmet. Behind him is a trench with other soldiers observing enemy positions. One soldier appears to be looking through a 6 x 30 Sf 14Z Scherenfernrohr (scissor binoculars).

(**Above**) Support vehicles parked in a wooded area to conceal themselves against ground or aerial surveillance. Note the divisional insignia of Wiking painted in white on the mudguards of two support vehicles. The other vehicle is a light Horch cross-country car and is being serviced by field mechanics.

(**Opposite, above**) An interesting photograph showing a Wiking camp during operations on the Eastern Front. The soldiers have turned their Zeltbahn shelter quarters into tents. The Zeltbahn was first issued in 1931 and was carried by each German soldier as part of his personal equipment. It was a very popular multipurpose piece of equipment. It could be used as a poncho, it protected the wearer's service uniform from getting wet, it could be used as personal camouflage or for camouflaging equipment, and it could be used to construct multi-person shelters, as this photograph clearly shows.

(**Opposite, below**) A column of Wiking troops on the march in October 1941. A number of Horch light cross-country vehicles can be seen with motorcyclists in support negotiating a typical road through the Russian countryside.

Two photographs showing Wiking support vehicles advancing along a muddy road. In late 1941 the supply situation was worsened by the almost non-existence of proper roads. Halftracks and other tracked vehicles were used to help speed up the supply of ammunition and other equipment desperately required at the front.

Two photographs showing the perilous advance of Army Group South in the autumn of 1941 as vehicles negotiate a muddy road. Due to the appalling road conditions the use of the main roads was restricted generally to priority class vehicles such as tanks and halftracks. Next in priority came the ammunition columns and fuel convoys, and then the reinforcements needed to nourish the advance. The nearer to the battle zones, the worse the road system became.

(**Opposite, above**) Motorcyclists struggle with their motorcycle combination as it tries to advance along a muddy road. In western Russian the roads had not been constructed to carry the amount and weight of traffic that now used them, and the surfaces began to break up under the strain. Even after a short downpour the roads in central Russia could be turned in to a slurry, often bringing progress to a crawl or standstill.

(**Above**) A prime mover has thrown a track and sits on a muddy road outside a Russian village in the autumn of 1941. The successful performance of the German army on the battlefield was attributed mainly to the halftrack, that transported troops, ordnance and supplies to the front. These front-wheel steering vehicles with tracked drive transformed the army's fighting ability during the Second World War.

(**Opposite, below**) Halftracks belonging to Kleist's 1st Panzer Army towing artillery to the front in the Rostov area in November 1941. Division Wiking supported the 1st Panzer Army's evacuation of Rostov and fell back over the Mius River, some 60 miles west of the city.

The crew of an 8.8cm Flak gun supporting Division Wiking and the 1st Panzer Army's withdrawal across the Mius River in December 1941. Both the 1st Panzer Army and the Wiking Division were ordered to hold their battered and frost-bitten forces behind the Mius at all costs. Although its forces had been forced to withdraw across the river, it was a tactical success and in fact saved ground, but at an alarming expenditure in men and material.

Two Panzer men from the 1st Panzer Army pose for the camera in front of their Pz.Kpfw.IV during operations along the Mius River with the Wiking Division during the winter of 1941.

Behind the Mius River Wiking troops are clad in winter sheepskin greatcoats to protect themselves from the arctic temperatures in late 1941. The soldier armed with a Karabiner 98K bolt action rifle is more than likely on guard duties.

(**Above**) Two photographs showing Pz.Kpfw.IVs from the 1st Panzer Army advancing across the snow during the Mius Front operation. The 1st Panzer Army included the III, XIV and XLVIII Army Corps (motorized) with five panzer divisions and four motorized divisions (two of them SS, including the Wiking Division), equipped with 799 tanks.

(**Opposite, above**) Troops move across the snow with a sled of supplies during winter operations on the Eastern Front in 1941. The men are wearing snow suits that consisted of a white jacket and white trousers. Although the Wiking Division sustained heavy casualties during the winter of 1941, they held the line, and by early 1942 a stalemate with the Russians had developed. Before spring, only minor skirmishes continued as both sides rebuilt their strength.

(**Opposite, below**) There were more than 800,000 horses on the Eastern Front in 1941, and some 8,000 a day were being killed, by enemy fire, the extreme arctic temperatures and overexertion. In this photograph the SS are using horses to pull supplies through the snow.

(**Above**) A well concealed 2cm Flak gun positioned in the snow during winter operations in 1941. This weapon was the primary German light anti-aircraft gun, and by far the most numerous German artillery piece used throughout the war.

(**Opposite, above**) Division Wiking on the move on an icy road in late 1941. A motorcyclist leads a column of support vehicles towards the front.

(**Opposite, below**) Red Army soldiers captured along the Mius River have been assembled before evacuation to the rear. Most of them are dressed in greatcoats and wear the shapka-ushanka, the synthetic fur pile or felt, ear-flapped cap introduced in 1940.

A Flak gunner can be seen wearing a sheepskin vest over his tunic to keep his torso protected against the arctic temperatures.

Here an SS soldier wears another form of winter camouflage, the snow overall. An early piece of snow clothing, it was long, covering the entire service uniform, and designed to reach the wearer's ankles. It was shapeless, had buttons right down the front, and had a deep collar, attached hood and long sleeves. The infantryman's black leather belt and personal equipment was normally worn attached around the outside of the garment to allow better access, but it is concealed by this soldier. He is also wearing the cold-weather headdress: helmet toques that were a tight-fitting camouflage reversible hood designed to be worn under the steel helmet as part of the winter uniform. He can be seen armed with stick grenade, which has been placed in his pocket.

An SS soldier, more than likely posted for guard duties in the snow. The man wears the fur-lined animal skin greatcoat. This was known as a 'Wachmantel' (guard overcoat) or 'Steppenmantel' (Steppe overcoat). These warm coats were issued not only to guards but also to vehicle drivers.

A patrol leader clad in his winter whites is about to lead a patrol. He is armed with an MP38/40 machine gun. He wears a whitewashed M35 steel helmet and beneath the helmet his head is protected by a toque. This close-fitting headdress was primarily designed for warmth and was made of either wool or cloth.

(**Opposite, above**) An Sd.Kfz.10/4 with a mounted 2cm Flak gun positioned in the snow during the 1st Panzer Army's Mius operation in late 1941. Onboard the halftrack, the side gun platform has been folded down to provide additional space for the crew to manoeuvre around the gun.

(**Above**) An interesting photograph showing an unidentified SS Wiking unit during a defensive action along the Mius River in the winter of 1941. All the soldiers are clad in their winter uniforms and wear rifle ammunition pouches. They have all been issued with the Karabiner 98K rifle. By the look of the discarded ammunition boxes, there has been some heavy fighting.

(**Opposite, below**) Here in the snow during defensive operations along the Mius River is a 21cm Mörser 18 (21cm Mrs 18), or 21cm Mörser M 18/L31 on tow in the snow. This weapon was a heavy howitzer used by independent artillery battalions and batteries. It was powerful, had a long range, and was mounted in a 'mortar style' carriage that allowed very high elevation.

On guard duties and this SS infantryman, armed with Karabiner 98K rifle and stick grenade, is seen wearing the animal skin greatcoat over his army field service uniform. This garment was very effective against the sub-zero temperatures on the Eastern Front.

(**Opposite, above**) This SS infantryman, probably on patrol, is wearing a snow coverall, winter boots, and is armed with a Karabiner 98K bolt action rifle. Around his neck he is wearing 6 x 30 field binoculars. Snow camouflage smocks and coveralls were originally used by ski and mountain troops before the war. During the first winter months on the Eastern Front white camouflage became a necessity and SS divisions were supplied with thousands of improvised winter garments.

(**Opposite, below**) An interesting photograph showing SS troops still wearing their summer camouflage smocks, and regular Wehrmacht soldiers wearing their standard army greatcoats and M38 field caps in the snow in 1941. All they have done to protect themselves from the low temperatures is to wear woollen toque and mittens.

An interesting photograph showing an SS column of vehicles following a line of Russian soldiers with horses and carts. It appears that this Red Army column is moving the carts to the rear so that the Germans can press them into service.

In a defensive position along the Mius River and this soldier, wearing a Wehrmacht greatcoat, is armed with a Karabiner 98K bolt action rifle. His equipment is the enlisted man's army leather belt, a pair of ammunition pouches, M1931 bread bag, M1931 field flask with drinking cup, M1931 mess kit, S84/98 bayonet with leather frog, and a small entrenching tool.

Chapter Two

Battles in Southern Russia

After enduring the first Russian winter of 1941–42 and holding the line behind the Mius, Wiking was ordered to retake Rostov-on-Don and thrust into the Caucasus securing the region's oilfields. This attack, code-named Operation Mius, formed a part of Army Group South's new summer offensive called Case Blue. It was an ambitious plan that involved the seizure of Stalingrad, and the isthmus between the Don and the Volga. Following the capture of Stalingrad the Germans planned to use the city as an anchor and send the mass of its force south to occupy the Caucasus, where it would be used to cut off Russian oil supplies.

The directive was executed in two stages. The first part of the summer operation was a determined all-out drive in successive enveloping thrusts along the Kursk-Voronezh axis, where it was to destroy the Soviet southern flank and follow through to the Don River. The second part was the advance to Stalingrad and across the lower Don into the Caucasus. For this operation Army Group South would be divided: General List's Army Group A South would advance towards Rostov and the Caucasus, and General von Weichs' Army Group B would be responsible for the drive across the lower Don to the Volga and into Stalingrad.

For the summer offensive several divisions, especially those spearheading the drive, were brought to authorized strength levels, which included artillery, anti-tank and anti-aircraft weapons. German strength in the air was equalled to that of the 1941 campaign with 1,500 aircraft of the total of 2,750 being sent down to the southern sector of the front.

Over the following few weeks, strung out over more than 200 miles, the troops of Operation Blue pushed down towards the Don corridor on Stalingrad. The tremendous distances which these divisions had to cover could only be achieved by long foot marches. Natural obstacles such as the balka, which were high and steep-sided, dried-up watercourses, often obstructed the advance of a tank column until a diversion was made or a bridge erected. Some areas of the advance were hampered by lack of fuel, which had been temporarily diverted to Army Group A (Heeres Gruppe A). Despite the problems that faced the Wehrmacht, Wiking pushed forward and made good progress. Within six weeks Rostov and the entire Don region had been captured, and Wiking was advancing deep into the Caucasus.

In later September 1942, Wiking participated in the operation aimed to capture the city of Grozny, alongside the 13th Panzer Division. Initially the attack went well with the division capturing the town of Malgobek on 6 October, but due to the encirclement of the 6th Army at Stalingrad, all attempts by Wiking to reach Grozny with Panzer support were halted. Further advances into the Caucasus were also blunted.

By late November 1942, the Red Army had completed their plan of encircling some 300,000 Axis personnel in and around the battered and blasted city of Stalingrad in an operation known as Uranus. The forces trapped inside the city were too weak to break out and this led to Field Marshal Erich von Manstein undertaking a relief operation called Winter Storm. In mid-December Wiking, now redesignated as the 5th SS Panzergrenadier Division Wiking, was ordered to support the relief operation, but due to the snow and stiff enemy resistance, by the time it arrived at the end of December to join the operation, the division was forced to cover the withdrawal of Army Group A, which had been severely mauled. Over the coming days and weeks the division, with Army Group A, moved towards Rostov and escaped through what was known as the Rostov gap on 4 February 1943.

During this period Wiking was once again thrown into fierce fighting, this time to help in the recapture of Kharkov with other premier Waffen-SS divisions. The Kharkov area was regarded by both the German and Soviet forces as a pivotal area on the Eastern Front, sitting astride two important strategic axes towards Kursk and the Donbas. The Germans were determined capture the city. Wiking was immediately entrained towards the city with the 11th Panzer division, but ran into strong Russian forces. These forces were the Soviet Mobile Popov which was threatening to break through to a vital rail line. The division was ordered to hold this rail line at all costs, but its units were under strength and weak following weeks of battle in the Caucasus. Panzergrenadier regiments found it difficult to repulse the heavy Soviet armour, but in spite of their weakened condition, the division held on to grim death, protected the rail line and helped bring about the destruction of Mobile Group Popov. The loss of Popov's Group halted the Soviet offensive and stabilized Manstein's front, bringing relief to his tired and depleted troops.

In the face of adversity, the 5th SS Panzergrenadier Division Wiking had shown its worth on the battlefield and earned respect not just among the other Waffen-SS divisions, but in the whole of the Wehrmacht too.

During this period Wiking underwent major transformation. Herbert Gille was appointed commander and the SS Regiment Nordland, along with its commander Fritz von Scholz, was removed from the division and used to command the new 11th SS Volunteer Panzergrenadier Division Nordland. The Finnish Volunteer Battalion was also disbanded and replaced by the Estonian Infantry battalion Narwa.

During this period of expansion the Waffen-SS for the first time had finally resorted to the large-scale conscription of foreign recruits. Thousands of youths who met SS standards were now being drafted from the work camps of the Reich Labour Service. Nordic volunteers and Volksdeutsche – people of Germanic decent from countries in Eastern Europe – helped dilute the so-called pure Nordic stock with foreign blood. Over the next two years this expansion saw the final Waffen-SS order of battle of thirty-eight divisions, though the later divisions never approached the proper level of manpower. Foreign soldiers prominently manned many of these divisions. Only about twelve of the divisions were a true elite; most were formed late in the war and were divisions in name only, often being poorly equipped.

Between February and July 1943 the Waffen-SS saw a large expansion. The 9th SS-Panzergrenadier-Division 'Hohenstaufen' and the 10th SS-Panzergrenadier-Division 'Frundsberg' were being formed. In March, the 11th SS-Freiwilligen-Panzergrenadier-Division 'Nordland' was created by merging the four Germanic legions, units from the 5th SS-Division Wiking, and a large group of new west European recruits.

While best efforts were made to expand the Waffen-SS during the first half of 1943, the elite combat formations saw extensive action and were continuously being shuttled from one danger spot to another, with only brief rest for refitting. Wherever they were committed to battle, Wiking, along with the other SS Panzer and Panzer-grenadier divisions, attacked. Sometimes they were successful, sometimes they failed. But whatever the outcome of the action, the end mostly resulted in delaying the enemy advance. This had become the value of the Waffen-SS in the last two years of the war.

In these last years, the deciding factors in ground warfare were the Panzer, self-propelled artillery, and mechanized infantry. They had become such important factors in the successful prosecution of the war that seven of the thirty Panzer divisions and six Panzergrenadier divisions became elite Waffen-SS formations. The seven divisions became Hitler's emergency 'fire brigade', and had occasional assistance from a number of less elite SS-Panzergrenadier divisions.

Hitler looked upon these divisions to blunt the Soviet offensive that had gained the initiative following the destruction of the 6th Army at Stalingrad. As far as he was concerned, the SS had stood firm in the face of adversity – unlike the Wehrmacht.

In March 1943, Kharkov was recaptured by the elite SS divisions, Leibstandarte Adolf Hitler, Das Reich, and Totenkopf. After stemming the Soviets at Kharkov, the SS-Panzer-Korps were prepared to spearhead the German summer offensive on the central sector of the Eastern Front, around Orel and Kursk. This would be the last major offensive operation undertaken by the Germans in the east. What would follow would be almost two years of bitter, bloody defensive battles, with the Waffen-SS being rushed from one disintegrating sector of the front to another, plugging gaps and fighting to the death to slow down the inevitable advance of the Red Army.

(**Above**) An interesting photograph showing two Flak gunners wearing animal skin greatcoats standing beside their emplaced 2cm Flak 30. This gun weighed 770kg with an effective ceiling range of 2,200 metres against aerial targets.

(**Opposite, above**) Infantry march past a burning Russian vehicle during winter operations in early 1942. The men are kitted out with the early snow overalls. By this period of the war Army Group South began to demonstrate its renowned powers of recovery and was poised to gain the initiative in southern Russia.

(**Opposite, below**) The deadly 8.8cm Flak gun, which can be seen with a wooden wall camouflaging part of the emplacement. The 8.8cm Flak gun was often difficult to identify at long distances, especially when the crew had whitewashed the weapon.

(**Above**) An SS soldier dressed in his familiar winter jacket poses for the camera in front of a captured bunker. Note how dirty his white jacket has become.

(**Opposite, above**) An infantryman inside an emplacement probably overlooking enemy positions. He is armed with the Kar98K bolt action rifle which appears to be perched on top of the emplacement in a firing position. Note the crude cloth helmet cover.

(**Opposite, below**) An artillery observation post and a soldier wearing a white camouflage suit is using the 6 × 30 Sf.14Z Scherenfernrohr or scissor binoculars searching for enemy targets. In extreme conditions the lenses would sometimes ice over. Each artillery battery had an observation post.

(**Above**) From a snow-covered trench a soldier surveyors the battlefield through a pair of binoculars. His one-piece snow suit and whitewashed M1935 steel helmet blends in well with the winter surroundings.

(**Opposite, above**) The crew of an 8.8cm Flak gun struggle through the snow with their weapon. During 1942 the Germans began pressing into service an amazing variety of requisitioned civil vehicles and purpose-built military vehicles to pull their guns. Although tracked vehicles generally towed the 8.8cm Flak gun, mud and deep snow usually hampered movement.

(**Opposite, below**) An officer converses with two SS men on a snowy road. Units of Wiking continued to fight hard to hold their positions despite being constantly subject to intense bombardments by Soviet artillery.

During a patrol ski troops halt inside a forest. The soldier on the left, wearing a two-piece snow suit, woollen toque and whitewashed steel helmet, is armed with an MP38/40 sub-machine gun. Signs of enemy movement were often easier to identify in the snow, and a vigilant patrol could quickly detect the location of their enemy by fresh foot prints, and snow knocked off bushes.

Weary infantry rest and eat their rations after enduring perhaps many days of bitter fighting against advancing Russian forces. The troops are compelled to protect themselves against the bitter temperatures with Zeltbahn shelter-quarters. Foliage from the surrounding pine trees has been used as bedding.

(**Above**) A heavily laden ski-mounted patrol moves forward out of some woodland. Unusually much of their personal kit and equipment has not been camouflaged against the white background.

(**Opposite**) Two photographs showing mainly infantry posing for the camera beside a log constructed building. They are wearing snow camouflage smocks and hooded overalls. Many of the men are wearing thick woollen gloves and a woollen toque for the head. Their M1935 steel helmets are painted with whitewash.

(**Opposite, above**) An interesting photograph showing resting troops wearing their snow overalls, woollen mittens and specially-manufactured winter felt over boots, which were originally a design of Russian origin. Note the excellent display of all the infantryman's combat equipment hanging from part of the log constructed building. Three Kar98k carbine bolt action rifles can also be seen.

(**Above**) Heavy fighting in Army Group South and these gunners are preparing their 8.8cm Flak gun for a fire mission in the snow. Note the loader holding one of the 9.4kg projectiles. The 8.8cm Flak's high velocity and flat trajectory made it a very accurate and effective weapon in both anti-tank and anti-aircraft roles.

(**Opposite, below**) An SS MG34 light machine gunner can be seen on the march across a snowy field supported by a Pz.Kpfw.III tank which appears to be transporting other troops towards the front. Each infantry group possessed an MG34 light machine gun, around which its base of fire was built.

(**Opposite, above**) In another winter setting and infantrymen dressed in cold weather and snow camouflage garments can be seen with animals beside a stockpile of ammunition cases. Out in the open like this, units were easily spotted by enemy reconnaissance aircraft, and suffered devastating attacks by Soviet bombers and artillery.

(**Above**) An infantryman probably on local security patrol. Artillery units were expected to provide their own local security and defence.

(**Opposite, below**) In the snow an infantryman is posted as an air guard standing next to an MG34 machine gun mounted on a MG34 anti-aircraft tripod mount.

(**Opposite, above**) After spending a period of time encamped in a snow-covered field German troops begin packing their equipment onto sleds to continue their march. Frequently soldiers found moving through snow on foot difficult and exhausting, but the sled was one of the most convenient forms of transportation through the snow.

(**Above**) Wiking soldiers hitching a lift aboard the engine deck of a whitewashed Pz.Kpfw.IV. Some of the soldiers appear to be sleeping, worn down from the fighting, bitter cold and miles of trudging through the snow.

(**Opposite, below**) Infantrymen wearing their winter reversibles grey side out are assisting a column of horse drawn transport through the thick snow. Even in late 1942 most of the motive power used by the SS was animal draught. Many hundreds of thousands of animals died either due to combat action, the extreme weather, lack of forage, or they were eaten by starving soldiers.

Infantry on a patrol inside a forest during winter operations in 1942. Troops that fought in the first winter in Russia made many sacrifices and those that managed to survive the ordeal got a medal to prove they had been there. They nicknamed the decoration the 'Frozen Meat Medal'.

SS troopers on a light Horch cross-country car wear a two-piece snowsuit. One soldier is armed with a Kar 98k bolt-action rifle which has received an application of winter whitewash paint. With the Red Army forces wearing similar winter clothing, front line German troops were normally issued with coloured armbands enabling them to distinguish between friend and foe. These soldiers wear black arm bands.

A light machine gun crew with their MG34 in the depths of the Russian winter of 1942 tucking into their rations. The troops have discarded their M1935 steel helmets to eat.

Out on patrol, troops can be seen taking cover while their troop leader surveys the terrain through binoculars.

During the spring of 1942 a heavy MG34 machine gun troop are seen on the march. Heavy machine guns were normally found in the three platoons of the grenadier battalion's machine gun company. Each platoon had four machine guns organized into two two-gun groups.

A projectile is being placed inside the 5cm barrel of the leGrW 36 mortar. A trenching tool has clearly been used to place the mortar into the soil to make it level for firing. The leGrW 36's intended role was to engage pockets of resistance that were beyond the range of hand grenades. It was designed for high angled fire only (no less than 42°). The main drawbacks of the weapon were its inadequate range and the limited effectiveness of its ammunition, which was regarded as not heavy enough.

An MG34 being prepared for a fire mission. This machine gun could be used in both a light and heavy role and had an effective range of 2,000 metres. It also had an impressive rate of fire of 800–900 rounds per minute. This weapon could deliver a formidable volume of fire and was particularly effective at combating low level aircraft attacks.

Three photographs taken during a training session showing a soldier armed with the deadly Flammenwerfer 35, or FmW35, a one-man flamethrower primarily used to clear out trenches and buildings. It weighed 35.8 kilograms, held 11.8 litres of fuel, and could project burning fuel 25 metres. The fuel was a mixture of petrol and tar to make it heavier and stickier. It was ignited by a hydrogen torch and provided about ten seconds of constant use.

(**Above**) An independent mobile maintenance unit inside a wooded area on the Eastern Front in the summer of 1942. These maintenance units were the lifeblood of the division and ensured that the vehicles were being kept in working order.

(**Opposite**) Wiking troops taking cover along an embankment during Operation Rostov in the summer of 1942. This photograph was taken outside the city before its capture. When Rostov fell the division recuperated and was reorganized comprising the SS Nordland Regiment, the I/SS Germania Regiment, SS Panzer Abteilung 5, 1 Engineer company, SS AR4 (artillery), AA Abteilung (Flak), 1 Reconnaissance company, 1 Panzer Jäger Abteilung, and support units comprising communications, maintenance and supply. The Kampfgruppe was split into three groups comprising 1 Infantry battalion, 1 Artillery group, 1 AA platoon and anti-tanks.

(**Opposite, above**) Assault troops taking cover on the vast steppe during the Rostov operation. This photograph is an excellent display of an infantryman's combat equipment. They have been issued with the usual rifleman's equipment and weapons including the 7.92mm Mauser Kar98k carbine. In their kit they have rifle ammunition pouches, a small entrenching tool, an S84/98 bayonet with leather frog, M1931 bread bag, M1931 field flask with drinking cup, M31 mess kit, M31 Zeltbahn shelter quarter and M1924 stick grenades. The soldier on the left is part of a machine gun squad and can be seen carrying full kit and MG34 ammunition boxes. These boxes contained either six 50-round belts (300 rounds) linked together, or a single 250-round belt.

(**Opposite, below**) Assault troops preparing to march, supported by halftracks.

(**Above**) MG34 assault troops on the march through a field supported by heavy armour. Two of the soldiers on the right can be seen carrying the Laufbehalter 34 container for two spare machine gun barrels; the similar Laufschützer 34 carried only a single spare barrel. One of the men carries an MG34 ammunition box on his back.

Smiling for the camera these Wiking troops in full battle kit pose on board the engine deck of a tank while being transported from one position on the front to another. One of the soldiers is armed with an MG42 machine gun, while his comrade next to him, a Scharführer (squad leader), is armed with an MP40 sub-machine gun. This gun was manufactured from 1941 in greater numbers and issued to squad leaders, senior NCOs and front-line officers.

(**Opposite, above**) A light MG42 machine gun team during operations in Russia in 1942. The gun's bipod can be seen extended. Under battlefield conditions the bipod would invariably be extended when carried and the belt loaded so that the gunner could quickly throw it to the ground and put it into operation. The dependability of the MG42 was second to none and every unit of the Waffen-SS and German army was equipped with it.

(**Opposite, below**) In a trench during a firing mission with a heavy MG42.

Mortar troops rest during a pause in the fighting with their well-dug-in 8cm sGrW 34.

In mid-December 1942 Wiking was redesignated as the 5th SS Panzergrenadier Division Wiking. At the end of December it was severely mauled by strong Russian forces as it withdrew towards Rostov. In this photograph, winter clad Wiking troops armed with an MG34 are seen out in an icy field. In the distance Pz.Kpfw.IVs can be seen in battle formation preparing for a fire mission.

(**Above**) In action during the early winter of 1943 is a soldier armed with the Flammenwerfer 41, or FmW 41, which was the standard German flamethrower introduced in 1941 and was an upgraded version of the earlier Flammenwerfer 35. It was designed to clear enemy trenches and buildings in highly fortified areas.

(**Opposite, above**) A group of troops clad in their winter whites on the march in single file, armed with the light MG42. In open terrain an MG42 machine gun squad would often use their sustained fire-mount to protect the flanks of the advancing rifle companies. However, in built-up areas or where crews were required to move quickly from one position to another the machine gunners often had to operate forward with the rifle platoons and in light machine gun roles with bipods only. They were still able to take advantage of the situation and revert to the heavy machine gun role if necessary.

(**Opposite, below**) Two soldiers wearing white camouflage snow overalls stand beside their whitewashed 5cm PaK 38 in a defensive position surrounded by earth and snow. The PaK 38 was well liked amongst the SS crews. Not only was the weapon effective in combat, but it was also easy to conceal.

(**Opposite, above**) In a firing position is a whitewashed modified 10.5cm le.FH18/42, and artillerymen wearing the two-piece reversibles white side out. The 10.5cm was the standard light artillery piece deployed in the artillery divisions on the Eastern Front and they were to be found in many of the SS divisions. To give the gun a bigger punch on the battlefield the weapon was modified in 1942. The barrel was lengthened, a cage muzzle brake was fitted, and the carriage became a lightened version of the le.FH 18 design.

(**Above**) Out in the field during Wiking's withdrawal through what was known as the Rostov gap in southern Russia, is a stationary whitewashed Tiger tank which has winter clad soldiers hitching a lift.

(**Opposite, below**) Out in the field is a six-barrelled Nebelwerfer 41 multiple rocket launcher. In order to try to conceal the weapon the crew have applied foliage over the rocket tubes and ammunition cases, which can be seen dangerously placed beneath the launcher. After the crew had loaded and aimed the launcher, they would take cover a few metres away and fire the Nebelwerfer remotely with an electric wire.

(**Above**) A photograph showing SS gunners with a 7.5cm PaK97/38 out in the snow being prepared for action. There were never enough PaK guns to meet the ever-increasing demand on the Eastern Front.

(**Opposite, above**) A common scene in southern Russia, even during the summer months when there was heavy rain. Here a motorcycle combination struggles through a field after rain has turned it into a quagmire. Dirt roads and fields were constantly being churned up which created even greater problems for vehicles following in the rear.

(**Opposite, below**) A Wiking MG42 light machine gun troop take cover in a trench to wait before going into action. In the distance two Pz.Kpfw.IV Ausf.G/Js can be seen rolling into battle. The soldiers wear their issued winter uniforms that include the grey parka with hoods lined with white fur.

Wiking Panzer troops during a pause in their march in southern Russia in 1943. Note the Pz.Kpfw.III with the divisional insignia of the Wiking division painted on the rear of the vehicle next to the national cross. A fuel drum has been attached to the rear of the tank to extend its range. Two of the crew sitting against the tank are wearing the sheepskin-lined grey winter anorak which was worn over their standard Waffen-SS field grey tunic. Their reversible winter trousers are grey side out and are tucked into a pair of marching boots. The other two men are wearing the black Panzer jacket. Their trousers are field grey vehicle uniform trousers that were identical to the black version and they are wearing them with a pair of black marching boots. They are wearing the M38 black panzer field cap which displays the death head badge.

Chapter Three

Kursk and Beyond

In early July 1943, the Waffen-SS were yet again put to the test in what was known as Operation Zitadelle, in the Kursk salient. It was here around Kursk that Army Group Centre had more or less maintained the strategic initiative on the Eastern Front, and it was for this prime reason that Hitler was confronted with a tempting strategic opportunity that he was convinced would yield him victory. This would be last great German offensive on the Eastern Front. The attack would be launched against a huge salient at Kursk measuring some 120 miles wide and 75 miles deep. However, the Soviets had already fortified the area with a massive array of mine belts, artillery, and tank traps. In front of this Soviet defensive fortress stood the cream of all the German combat formations, the premier divisions of the Waffen-SS. In Army Group South these elite soldiers were deployed for action, ready at a moment's notice to fight their way through the formidable lines of barbed wire entanglements, mine fields and anti-tank guns. Wiking, along with the 23rd Panzer Division, formed the reserve force for Manstein's Army Group for the operation.

Within two weeks of the Kursk offensive the Red Army had caused such massive losses to the German mobile units that they were compelled to withdraw from the Kursk salient to avoid complete annihilation.

By mid-August 1943, the Russians had wrenched open a huge gap in the German lines west of Kursk, once again threatening to retake Kharkov. Das Reich, Totenkopf and Wiking divisions were immediately thrown into battle to prevent the loss of the city. Although all the combat formations apart from Wiking were weakened by the offensive at Kursk, they were still a formidable fighting machine and determined to defend the city. The Red Army, however, wanted to recapture it and launched a massive pincer attack.

Within days of the SS redeployment to Kharkov, the Russian 53rd Army driving from north, and the 57th Army advancing from the south, attacked the city in full strength. Almost immediately the SS troops crashed into action and defended Kharkov with vigour and fortitude.

Fighting in and around the city intensified, and on 20 August Totenkopf and the Grossdeutschland division joined hands to close the gap west of the city. However, by this stage of the battle both divisions were running out of ammunition and were already relying heavily on artillery to undertake the main burden of defending their positions. The high consumption of ammunition in the last month had put serious strain on all the German combat formations in and around Kharkov. Units of Wiking for instance complained that daily supplies of artillery and tank ammunition were down to half the normal capacity required to sustain a force of such magnitude in a defensive position. Despite these problems they were told to hold the city and throw everything they could against the Soviets. But when they arrived in the 6th Corps zone of operations, they found that the artillerymen, after firing their last rounds, were abandoning their guns and fighting as infantry.

Fighting around the city was heavy. In one day of fighting SS anti-tank gunners knocked out nearly 200 Soviet tanks. The Das Reich Panther battalion, which first saw heavy combat on 22 August, destroyed 53 Russian tanks. The next day, just west of Kharkov, a Panther platoon broke up a Russian tank assault, and one Panther destroyed seven tanks. On 24 August, the 6th SS Panzer-Kompanie, newly supplied with the latest Panzer IVs, battled sixty Russian T-34 tanks between Udy-Bogens and Orkan, just south-west of the city, and knocked out twenty-nine of them. In the ten-day battle that raged around Kharkov the Das Reich division alone had scored 463 armoured kills.

Totenkopf and Wiking were equally impressive, and fought a series of skilful duels against numerically superior enemy forces. Again and again they showed their worth in the field of action. In spite of serious losses in men and material, the troops continued fighting with all the ruthlessness and élan that made them such an efficient and lethal weapon of war.

Through the latter part of August the SS continued to score some outstanding successes in localised combats with Russian armoured units. However, with acute shortages in men and equipment the situation deteriorated day by day. Despite frantic calls from commanders appealing for the evacuation from the city, Hitler sent out an order that Kharkov be held under all circumstances and demanded the most severe measures against any units that failed to execute their assigned missions. Waffen-SS units were forced to undertake their Führer's futile exercise of holding Kharkov to the death.

As the situation rapidly deteriorated and the hard-pressed soldiers became ground down against numerically superior forces, Hitler became increasingly worried that another Stalingrad would soon develop. By early September he grudgingly decided to allow the order to pull troops out of the doomed city. The Waffen-SS withdrew from Kharkov in a spirited fighting retreat towards the River Dnieper. Here the SS managed to halt the Russian onslaught towards the river, allowing Manstein's forces to retreat and redeploy. The Waffen-SS had helped avert a major disaster in the area and given Manstein a little time to reorganise the front from the inevitable disaster that was looming. The SS, together with the elite arm of Grossdeutschland, covered the general retreat to the river, before retiring to the western bank of the river. Manstein was well aware that his army group could no longer hold the Donetz Line, and therefore sought to withdraw and regroup his forces across the River Dnieper. Altogether some sixty-eight German divisions – 1.25 million men and over 2,000 tanks of Army Group South – were tasked with holding the river line at all costs. Opposing them was a Red Army almost double in size, and furnished with plenty of reserves in fresh men and equipment.

The River Dnieper was the second largest Russian river and the strongest natural defence line in western Russia. Adequately fortified and manned, the Dnieper would have certainly been an excellent defensive line, but Army Group South in September 1943 was not adequately fortified and manned. Also, when troops crossed the river during their withdrawal from Kharkov they were dismayed to find none of the impregnable fortifications constructed.

In the first ten days of October the Red Army launched an attack against German positions in the great bend of the river between Kremenchug and Zaporozhye. The attack began with a massive artillery preparation that pounded the German bridgehead. In less than an hour they had counted some 15,000 shell bursts in their sector.

German batteries replied in kind as far as they were able, but the main attack would fall on the infantry. By 15 October, the Russian 2nd Ukrainian Front, with a total of six armies, bulldozed its way through and crossed the river. During the next few days they poured divisions across the river and tore open the German-held front between the 8th Army and the left wing of the 1st Panzer Army. On 18 October troops took Pyatikhatka, 35 miles south of the Dnieper, and cut off the main railway lines to Dnepropetrovsk and Krivoi Rog. Russian forces were now driving straight for Krivoi Rog. The city of Krivoi Rog contained the supply and ammunition dumps for the Army Group South, and the locomotives there were a vital asset for the supply to the army group.

Manstein was determined that he could not allow the loss of Krivoi Rog and scraped together what he could muster to stem the Russian onslaught. However, the units of the SS were hard pressed and did not receive the supplies of fresh men and armour they had been promised. What followed was a massive counter-thrust with Wehrmacht and Waffen-SS troops using all available reserves and resources to bitterly contest the Russian advance. In the bloody battle the Germans, at great cost in men and material, managed to break up two Russian armoured corps and nine rifle divisions. The Red Army lost more than 300 tanks and 5,000 prisoners. The remaining Russian forces in the area staggered back towards the Dnieper, allowing the exhausted German combat formations to temporarily stabilise the front.

The troops were made fully aware of the significance of holding Krivoi Rog, and the outcome would be the deciding factor in the future operations of Army Group South in the Crimea.

Further north along the Dnieper, soldiers of Wiking had meanwhile been trying to prevent enemy forces from consolidating west of the river. SS troops had been battling Red Army forces throughout late August and September trying to stop the Russians establishing a bridgehead. Wiking fought with great losses of men and armour but fought on undeterred.

Throughout the weeks that ominously followed the German front lines were pulled further westwards, with both Waffen-SS and Wehrmacht units defending, attacking and counter-attacking as the situation demanded.

As the winter of 1943 approached, a feeling of despair and gloom gripped the German front lines. To many of the soldiers there was a dull conviction that the war was lost, and yet there was still no sight of its end. Being always outnumbered, perpetually short of fuel and ammunition, and having to constantly exert themselves and their machinery to the limits of endurance had a profound effect on morale at the front.

During the latter half of 1943 the equipment situation continued to deteriorate, especially in the Panzer units. This was a constant concern for the tacticians. The SS did receive tanks, artillery and assault guns, but this was in stark contrast to the enormous volume of armaments being produced by the Russians. Unlike the normal German soldier, the elite SS elite troops retained their fanatical determination on the battlefield. Against the growing Soviet menace they still proved to be first class formations. Seven SS divisions became Hitler's emergency 'fire brigade', being shuttled from one danger spot to another: Leibstandarte Adolf Hitler, Das Reich, Totenkopf, Wiking, Hohenstaufen, Frundsberg and Hitlerjugend. In October 1943 they were redesignated SS Panzer divisions.

The seven new divisions maintained and enhanced the military reputation of the Waffen-SS. As the Wehrmacht established defensive lines in the face of the advancing enemy, commanders counted on the aggressive and loyal striking force of the SS to snatch victory from defeat. The strength of Wiking was strengthened with the Walloon volunteer unit of the 5th SS-Sturmbrigade 'Wallonien', which was attached to the division under the command of Léon Degrelle. Although this new unit was subject to ridicule by many of the Wiking veterans, they proved their worth against the Russians, notably in a forest outside the town of Teklino.

Although Wiking and its new Wallonia unit had shown skill and tenacity in the face of overwhelming superiority, it was still being pushed back, along with Manstein's Army Group South including the 8th Army. Here forces had followed the Dnieper River in a desperate attempt to construct defensive positions. By 1 December 1943 the line had been broken and the Soviet Army crashed over the Dnieper in force. Wehrmacht and Wiking forces tried with little success to hold back the Soviet attack and Wiking forces, together with the 8th Army, were pushed back towards the city of Cherkasy.

Marshal Zhukov ordered 1st and 2nd Ukrainian Fronts to undertake wide sweeping encircling movements, using similar tactics that encircled the 6th Army at Stalingrad. Within days the Soviets had formed two armoured rings of encirclement: an inner ring around the pocket followed by destruction of the forces it contained, and an external ring to prevent the German relief formations from reaching the surrounded units. Despite repeated warnings from Manstein, Hitler refused to allow the exposed units to be pulled back. Instead the Wehrmacht, Luftwaffe formations, and soldiers of Wiking began fighting for their lives in what became known as the battle of the Korsun–Cherkasy Pocket.

An engineer laying a Tellermine 43. This mine was a circular steel-cased anti-tank blast mine and between March 1943 and the end of the war some 3.6 million Tellermine 43s were produced.

Two photographs taken in sequence showing Wiking troops on the march in the summer of 1943 advancing through a sunflower field. They are clad in their summer camouflage smocks. These fields were perfect cover and soldiers often carried binoculars to get their bearings and range on the enemy.

A Panzer commander can be seen looking at a map during his unit's advance in July 1943. Following the battle of the Kursk salient, the Russians had wrenched open a huge gap in the German lines to the west, putting massive strain on the Waffen-SS that were already badly depleted from the battle. However, because Wiking had been put in reserve for the battle, its combat formations were able to support Das Reich and Totenkopf in force.

Inside a trench in 1943 and Wiking troops pose for the camera after being decorated with the Iron Cross.

(**Above**) An SS Hauptscharführer seen on the right confers with other commanders and squad leaders in the field during summer operations in 1943. The men's equipment comprises Zeiss 6 x 30 binoculars, SS enlisted man's leather belt, black infantry support straps, rifleman's ammunition pouches, and MP38/40 magazine pouches. Note the squad leader armed with three M1924 stick grenades which have been secured inside his black leather belt. The SS Hauptscharführer has been issued with the brown leather belt which is being worn with a 9mm P38 Walther pistol holster.

(**Opposite, above**) Waffen-SS troops can be seen with supporting armour spread out across the Russian steppe in the summer of 1943. The vehicles have purposely spread themselves apart to minimise damage to their column and make themselves more difficult to attack.

(**Opposite, below**) A soldier belonging to a signals battalion using a field telephone. The signals battalion provided both field and radio communications support within the division, linking all subordinate units. Regiments and battalions had their own signals, but for internal communications. Telephone and radio troops were attached to all divisional units and laid wire and cable for telephone connections.

(**Above**) Wiking troops can be seen with a burning Russian vehicle. Throughout the latter part of the summer the division continued to score some outstanding successes in localised combats with Russian armoured units. However, with acute shortages in men and equipment the situation deteriorated day by day.

(**Opposite**) Inside a trench and this SS MG34 machine gun team tuck into their rations.

(**Below**) A camouflaged PaK gun trains its barrel across a field.

An excellent photograph showing a light MG34 machine gunner inside a typical MG position in a field. Note the 50-round drum magazine attached to the MG34. The view for the gunner from here must have offered a good opportunity for detecting enemy movement from some distance away.

SS soldiers capture a Russian soldier inside a foxhole. The soldier on the right is armed with a Luger P08 pistol, while the other holds a captured Russian PPSh-41 (pistolet-pulemyot Shpagina) drum magazine machine gun.

Sheltered in what appears to be a captured Russian position are three soldiers, two wearing winter whites and one in an animal-skin fur coat. They are all wearing the black woollen toques which are being worn under their M35 steel helmets which have white helmet covers instead of winter whitewash paint. The helmet cover was normally held in place by a drawstring tightened up under the helmet rim and tied off.

Two SS soldiers armed with the Kar98K bolt action rifle are in a trench during operations in the autumn of 1943. Both men are wearing the grey winter anorak with M38 field cap complete with death head insignia stitched on the front. Scattered along the trench and in easy reach are M1924 stick grenades, M31 field flask with drinking cup, M1931 canteen and bread bag.

A crew member from a halftrack is about to tow a four-wheeled vehicle along a muddy road. The towing capability of the halftrack ensured that troops and ordnance often got through to their destinations despite the terrible quality of the roads.

A motorcyclist wearing what appears to be a grey anorak caked in mud smiles with a commanding officer and his comrades.

A machine gunner is on the march in the autumn of 1943. The soldier wears what appears to be a standard Wehrmacht greatcoat with his summer Waffen-SS camouflage smock worn over the top. Attached to the soldier's support straps is a 50-round drum magazine, an M31 field flask, an M1931 canteen, and attached to his black leather belt are two rifle ammunition pouches and an MG toolbox. He wears around his neck 6 × 30 Zeiss binoculars.

Wiking Sd.Kfz.250 halftracks with mounted 2cm Flak guns are on the move through a decimated town in 1943. The Panzergrenadier behind the splinter shield in the leading halftrack wears the reversible winter suit with the grey side out. He is almost certainly wearing thick woollen gloves for handling the Flak gun and personal weapons.

Two grenadiers can be seen next to two support vehicles that still retain their summer camouflage colour scheme.

Inside a trench this light MG34 machine gunner is wearing a two-piece old snow suit. He is wearing a coloured armband on his right arm. Generally the colour armband was green, but it could be changed in colour or position depending on the frequently changing security sequence.

An SS PaK crew preparing their weapon for a fire mission against a Soviet target in the winter of 1943. Anti-tank weapons were integral to the martial prowess of the Waffen-SS and were an economical and effective counter to the firepower and mobility of enemy armour. They provided defensive staying power as SS troops found themselves confronted by ever-greater numbers of enemy tanks.

Chapter Four

Fighting for Survival

In early January 1944, Manstein's Army Group South had fallen back to the Panther-Wotan Line, a defensive position along the Dnieper River. At this point Soviet forces attempted to smash German forces around the town of Kirovograd. By 8 January the town fell, but the Russians soon found German resistance in the area stronger than expected. Some eleven German divisions, including the SS Wiking Division and the new Belgian Walloon volunteer unit, SS Sturmbrigade Wallonien, which had recently been transferred from the Wehrmacht to SS control, were embroiled in an attempt to stem the Soviet push westwards. These German divisions held a salient into the Soviet lines between the towns of Korsun and Cherkasy. Despite repeated warnings from Manstein, Hitler refused to allow the exposed units to be pulled back to safety.

On 18 January, Manstein was proved right when General Nikolai Vatutin's 1st and General Ivan Konev's 2nd Ukrainian Fronts attacked the forward lines of the salient and surrounded two German corps. Trapped in the Korsun pocket were 50,000 men, a total of six German divisions, including Wiking and Sturmbrigade Wallonien. The trapped forces were designated Gruppe Stemmermann, after their commander.

The Wiking division had some forty-three tanks and assault guns. Two assault gun battalions provided an additional twenty-seven assault guns. Wiking was the only armoured unit in the pocket, and with these tanks and assault guns they were ordered to drive the enemy back and transform an impossible situation by breaking out of the encirclement and destroying the enemy. Day and night the fighting raged, but the Russians, with some thirty-five divisions around the salient, inflicted terrible casualties. The constant pressure gradually saw the pocket shrink to some 40 square miles by early February.

On the night of 16 February, as the situation deteriorated to a point where it looked like every unit trapped in the pocket would be annihilated, Gruppe Stemmermann received a communiqué from Manstein ordering it to break out of the pocket at all costs. As German troops began to move slowly across the boggy terrain the Russians became aware of what was happening and opened up a massive barrage. Hundreds of Russian guns of all calibres poured a storm of fire onto the German positions. A Wiking soldier wrote later: 'The most fearsome sound of all came from the Katyushas or 'Stalin Organs'. These rocket machines with their distinctive shriek fired projectiles from 16-rail launchers miles into the enemy lines. Although it was not a precision weapon, it was hardly necessary if sixteen of them impacted in the same area. The terrifying noise they made was much feared by us, and the death and devastation they inflicted was terrible.'

Death and destruction inside the pocket was so severe that the wounded had to be left behind, as did most of the artillery and heavy equipment. SS Sturmbrigade Wallonien suffered terrible losses covering the rearguard, with almost three-quarters of its manpower left dead on the battlefield.

As the remnants pushed slowly forward nearer to the German lines, Russian fire intensified, inflicting even more casualties. In typical Waffen-SS style, the Wiking divisions' only remaining tanks turned back and fought to the death.

Das Reich was another combat formation that had been rushed to help relieve the troops in the pocket. They were among the rearguard units, holding fast while the bulk of the encircled troops made good their escape. Das Reich had suffered heavy losses as a result of their self-sacrifice. Out of 5,000 soldiers that were sent to the area some 1,121 of all ranks were killed in action.

In spite of the huge losses in men and equipment, some 33,000 German troops had escaped with their lives. Another disaster had been averted in southern Russia. The distinguished performances of the Waffen-SS had again increased its reputation as the foremost fighting machine on the Eastern Front. The Wiking commander Herbert Gille and SS-Hauptsturmführer Léon Degrelle, commander of the Walloons, were summoned to Hitler's East Prussian headquarters, the Wolfschanze, and decorated. Gille received the Oakleaves and swords, and Degrelle the Knight's Cross.

In spite of Gille's and Degrelle's brave attempts to divert a military catastrophe, the situation on the Eastern Front continued to worsen. By June 1944, German strategists were faced with a fully-fledged two-front war. More than 53 per cent of the army was fighting in Russia, while the other 47 per cent were now in Western Europe trying to stem the Allied invasion along the Normandy coast. On the Eastern Front, German Army strength had fallen to a new low of 2,240,000 men against more than 6 million Russian troops. The best-equipped and most effective segment of the German force, the Waffen-SS, consisted of some 400,000 men and of these most were fighting in France.

In the east the SS were distributed on all fronts and were intended to act as the backbone of the German fighting machine trying to hold the Red Army from rolling across into Poland, but it was all in vain. During July 1944 the Russians pushed forward and across the ravaged countryside of Poland through the shattered German front. Over the coming days and weeks fighting in southern Poland was fierce, with German divisions trying to organise a defence along the Vistula River. Totenkopf and Wiking divisions formed the 4th Panzer-Corps commanded by Herbert Gille. This corps was placed 30 miles northeast of Warsaw, where it was expected the renewal of the Russian offensive would begin.

Inside the Polish capital, as news spread that the Russians were drawing closer, the Polish Home Army suddenly revolted in what was known as the Warsaw uprising, and attempted to restore its sovereignty against the German invaders.

While the Warsaw uprising was being suppressed, the Russians attacked on 14 August northwest of the city and, for several bloody days, the well-dug-in Waffen-SS divisions of Wiking and Totenkopf grimly held out, repulsing a number of vicious attacks. The Red Army then regrouped and resumed their attack, and for four days SS troops held out. Russian air support hammered the German frontlines day and night until Wiking, Totenkopf and the rest of the Panzer corps withdrew from their battered and blasted positions west towards Warsaw.

By 10 September heavy fighting engulfed the suburbs of the city with the SS successfully defending its positions. For ten days, until the Red Army offensive petered out, the SS managed to hold their lines, in spite of high losses. During the next few weeks, until 10 October, there followed a lull in the fighting until the Russians launched yet another offensive, which forced the 4th Panzer Corps to retreat 20 miles westwards. By 27 October the front had once more stabilised and the Red Army abandoned further assaults against the 4th Panzer Corps. Calm returned to the front around Warsaw and Wehrmacht and Waffen-SS divisions tended to their wounded, re-equipped the best they could, and dug another defensive line.

Elsewhere on the Eastern Front the situation was equally dire. In the south Malinovsky's 2nd Ukrainian Front had broken through German defences, and the Red Army reached the Bulgarian border in early September. Within a week, Russian troops reached the Yugoslav frontier, and on 8 September 1944, Bulgaria and Romania declared war on Germany. By 23 September, Soviet forces arrived on the Hungarian border and immediately raced through the country for the Danube, reaching the river to the south of Budapest.

It was here in Hungary that Hitler placed the utmost importance on defending what he called the last bastion of defence in the east. Against all military logic, he felt that it was Hungary and not the Vistula River in Poland which presented a natural barrier against an advance on Germany. For the defence of Hungary he decided to use his premier Waffen-SS divisions, including Totenkopf and Wiking, that were positioned along the Vistula River.

On 26 December, the 6th Panzer-Corps, comprising Totenkopf and Wiking, were transferred from the Warsaw area and ordered to relieve Budapest. Fighting around the Hungarian capital was fierce and unrelenting. Soldiers of the Wiking Division fought in atrocious conditions, and were being slowly bled to death from Red Army attacks. By the end of January both Wiking and Totenkopf had suffered almost 8,000 casualties, including over 200 officers injured or killed.

On 13 February, the badly mauled Wiking was ordered away from Budapest and moved west to Lake Balaton to take up another defensive position. It was here that the 6th SS Panzer Army were ordered to hold positions to the last man in what was known as Operation Spring Awakening. However yet again, in spite a number of crack Waffen-SS divisions fighting fiercely to hold the front, the Red Army smashed its way through the German defences and wrenched open a gap more than 60 miles wide.

Within ten days of the Red Army opening its counter-offensive it had pushed its way through the Vertes mountains across three major rivers and had smashed the German formations opposing it. Although Wiking retreated into Czechoslovakia, Gille's units still remained as a support to the 6th SS Panzer Army. In the face of unrelenting attacks, Wiking performed a holding operation on the left flank of the 6th Panzer Army in the area between Lake Velence and Székesfehérvár. However, the Red Army were too powerful and forced back the German front with heavy casualties. Wiking did what it could to protect withdrawing Panzer and infantry forces as it fell back under a storm of fire.

Remnants of the division withdrew towards Vienna, where it fought to the bitter end to defend the city. It was here that the Wiking division, with its predominantly western European troops, were annihilated. What was left of the division escaped to surrender to American forces near Fürstenfeld on 9 May 1945.

(**Opposite, above**) Wiking Panzergrenadiers out in the frozen plains of southern Russia near the Dnieper River in January 1944. It was here that Manstein's Army Group South had fallen back to the Panther-Wotan Line, a defensive position along the Dnieper River. Strong Soviet forces smashed German forces around the town of Kirovograd, which fell on 8 January, but the Russians soon found German resistance in the area stronger than expected. Some eleven German divisions, including the SS Wiking division and the new Belgian Walloon volunteer unit (SS Sturmbrigade Wallonien) which had recently been transferred from the Wehrmacht to SS control, were embroiled in a drastic attempt to stem the Soviet push westwards.

(**Opposite, below**) Wiking and regular forces are seen spread out across a snowy field with armoured support near the Dnieper River in January 1944.

(**Opposite, above**) Troops of the SS-Freiwilligen Wallonien with Wiking soldiers during winter operations in the Ukraine in early 1944. The Walloon Legion served in the Wehrmacht and later in the Waffen-SS on both front line and reserve duties. In late December 1943 the Red Army launched the Dnieper–Carpathian offensive, with the objective of clearing the area west of the Dnieper. The Wallonien and Wiking, along with eleven other German divisions of 1st Panzer Army and 8th Army, were positioned in a salient on the western bank of the river where they clashed with Russian forces. What followed was bitter and bloody fighting as the Wallonien and Wiking units held their positions to the death.

(**Above**) An SS Flak position during a fire mission against an enemy target. These Flak gunners are wearing the reversible winter suits grey side out. Like so many of the troops during this later period, they have discarded the unpopular winter suit padded toque.

(**Opposite, below**) An SS Flak gunner surveying the terrain ahead trying to deduce the location of the enemy through a pair of 6 × 30 binoculars. The weapon next to him is a 5cm Flak gun, regarded as medium range. Note the kill markings painted either in white or yellow on the gun's splinter shield, indicating the number of aircraft or ground targets knocked out of action.

Three photographs showing quadruple Flak gun mounts. This lethal weapon could unleash a hurricane of fire at a rate of 1,800 rounds per minute. It had two operators, one who fired the top left and bottom right guns while the other fired the top right and bottom left guns. The loader could quickly change the magazines while the other continued to fire. Unfortunately for the Germans, there were too few of them or they were too dispersed to make any significant impact on the main Soviet operations which were already capturing or encircling many of the key towns and cities in the Ukraine.

(**Above**) Waffen-SS troops watch a 15cm Schweres Infanteriegeschütz 33 (Sf) auf Panzerkampfwagen 38(t) pass its position. This self-propelled vehicle, known as the Grille (cricket), was based on the CzechPz.Kpfw.38(t) and mounted the powerful 15cm s.IG 33 infantry gun. A total of 200 of these were produced, and there were two variants built, the Ausf.H and Ausf.K. They were both to serve in the Schweres Infanteriegeschütz companies within the Panzergrenadier regiments inside the Panzer and Panzergrenadier divisions. Each detachment had six available.

(**Opposite, above**) Wiking troops pose for the camera with a Polish woman in front of a support vehicle at a training camp in Chelm in the summer of 1944. They wear their distinctive summer camouflage M44 pea dot smocks with M44 camouflaged field caps.

(**Opposite, below**) Onboard a halftrack, Wiking grenadiers can be seen advancing across a field in Poland during defensive operations in the summer of 1944. Mounted on the front of the Sd.Kfz.251 is an MG42 machine gun.

(**Opposite, above**) During operations in the defence of Poland in July 1944 and Wiking soldiers can be seen with a camouflaged Marder tank destroyer. Wiking was sent to Poland in July where it fought along the River Vistula and took part in the crushing of the Warsaw uprising.

(**Opposite, below**) With the aid of a map a commanding officer converses with armoured crew members of a motorized infantry division in the summer of 1944. They wear the Dot 44 uniform in the Erbsenmuster camouflage pattern, also known as Pea pattern or Pea Dot camouflage. This two piece uniform was made from top-quality herringbone twill in the correct coarse cloth which was a mix of linen and rayon printed in dot camouflage. On their uniforms they have the usual Waffen-SS and rank insignia. Their head gear is the standard Panzer field cap with death head insignia to the front.

(**Above**) Out on patrol in a field during a reconnaissance mission and a radio operator can be seen with his radio equipment and what appears to be a field telephone. The signalman is operating a portable radio (Tornisterfunkgerät or TornFu). This radio piece was the standard radio system used at battalion and regimental level.

In Poland during summer operations in 1944 and a Waffen-SS10.5cm le.FH18/42 infantry gun crew are in action. The 10.5cm was the standard light artillery piece deployed in the artillery divisions on the Eastern Front – as seen previously. Throughout the war the 10.5cm provided troops with a versatile, relatively mobile, base of fire.

In a trench on a field telephone this Wiking soldier is relaying messages back through his chain of command. In the background are Panther tanks on the move across a field sporting an extensive summer camouflage scheme.

Two Sd.Kfz.2 on patrol in Poland. These tracked vehicles were known as the Kleines Kettenkraftrad HK 101 or Kettenkrad. Initially this vehicle was used as a motorcycle tractor for airborne units or Fallschirmjäger. With its overlapped and interleaved road wheels it was used extensively throughout the war mainly on the Eastern Front. There were two variants of the vehicle, the Sd.Kfz.2/1 and Sd.Kfz.2/2. Both were used with a trailer and had field communication gear mounted behind the driver. They were primarily tasked with laying communication cable from a special mounted wire spool. However the vehicle was versatile and was used for a variety of other tasks such as pulling medium-heavy loads and carrying troops quickly to new positions.

A column of Wiking troops on the march along a road. In August 1944 the Germans managed to gain strength and reorganise their defensive positions along the Vistula. The SS Totenkopf and Wiking divisions formed the 4th Panzer Corps commanded by SS-Gruppenführer Herbert Gille. This corps was placed 30 miles north-east of Warsaw where the new Russian offensive was expected to begin.

(**Above**) In a Polish farmstead these Wiking soldiers, clad in their Dot 44 camouflage smocks, appear to be retrieving something from a hidden trunk buried in the ground. They wear a host of equipment from a P38 pistol hard shell holster, to rifle ammunition pouches for their Karabiner 98K bolt action rifles, 6 x 30 binoculars, and map case.

(**Opposite, above**) In a trench during operations in Poland and two Wiking soldiers can be seen looking across the battlefield. A number of Russian tanks appear to have been knocked out of action, and two soldiers can be seen surveying one tank standing on its engine deck.

(**Opposite, below**) A 4-wheel Sd.Kfz.222 reconnaissance vehicle. This armoured car was a heavier version of the Sd.Kfz.221 and carried a 2cm KwK 30 cannon and a co-axial 7.92mm MG34 mounted in its 10-sided, open-topped rotating turret. Note the wire mesh hood protecting the turret top against grenade attacks.

(**Opposite, above**) Wiking troops inside a shallow trench during summer operations in Poland in 1944. In front of their position a number of StuG.IIIs are on the advance through a sunflower field.

(**Opposite, below**) A Wiking grenadier surveys the terrain standing next to a stationary StuG.III.Ausf.F/8 in the summer of 1944. Although the StuG (Sturmgeschütz) had provided attacking infantry fire support, during the latter part of the war the assault gun was continually hard pressed on the battlefield and constantly called upon for offensive and defensive fire support, where it was gradually compelled to operate increasingly in an anti-tank role.

(**Above**) A Wiking crew load 7.5cm ammunition shells onto a Panther tank during operations in Poland. Wiking's real striking power lay in the Panther Abteilung.

(**Opposite, above**) A Volkswagen 166 Schwimmwagen from III Abteilung SS Panzergrenadier Regiment Germania approaching an Sd.Kfz.251/1 halftrack from the same unit. Behind that is a Panther tank from the SS Panzer-Regiment 5 Wiking.

(**Above**) A great photograph taken from inside an Sd.Kfz.251 halftrack next to a Panther tank during summer operations in Poland in 1944. Both vehicles belong to the II Abteilung SS Panzergrenadier Regiment photographed east of Warsaw.

(**Opposite, below**) A motorcycle combination unit is pictured here in Poland driving through a burning village. While Russian strength was mounting daily, the Waffen-SS put up stiff resistance against the Red Army onslaught.

Moving through a field is a Panzergrenadier pictured wearing a summer camouflage M44 pea dot smock with M44 camouflaged field cap.

A photograph of a Panther II 02 belonging to Panzer-Regiment 3 of the SS Totenkopf Division which was part of the advanced elements fighting alongside the Wiking Division east of Warsaw during this period in the summer of 1944.

A commander belonging to the III SS Panzergrenadier-Regiment Germania examines the barrel of a knocked-out Russian SU-78 self-propelled tank during operations east of Warsaw.

Wiking troops examine a knocked-out Russian ISU-152 self-propelled gun. It was officially nicknamed by the Red Army as the 'Beast Killer' and was built in direct response to heavier German tanks like the Tiger and the Panther. The ISU-152 had no turret and crews found the gun difficult to aim. Because of this the ISU-152 was primarily used as mobile artillery to support infantry and armoured attacks.

A Panther tank belonging to 8 Kompanie SS Panzer-Regiment 5 and a halftrack from the III Abteilung SS Panzergrenadier Regiment 9 Germania during operations east of Warsaw in August 1944. Standing between the vehicles is Hauptsturmführer Karl Nicolussi-Leck. He was commander of the 2 Kompanie 5 SS Panzer Abteilung.

Panzergrenadiers tuck into their rations during the autumn of 1944 in Poland. Four of the soldiers wear the sheepskin-lined grey winter anorak. Their personal equipment is typical of a rifleman during this period. Note the variation of head gear.

During operations in Poland Panzergrenadiers stand next to a whitewashed StuG in late 1944. By the beginning of November tank strength in the Wiking division was badly depleted, down to only fifteen Panthers, seven Pz.Kpfw.IVs and a handful of Sturmgeschütz assault guns. Due to the losses, part of SS Panzer-Regiment 5 was sent to training in Lodz.

Wiking troops hitch a lift aboard a Sturmgeschütz assault gun during operations in Hungary in 1945. On 26 December 1944, the 6th Panzer-Corps, comprising Totenkopf and Wiking, were transferred from the Warsaw area and ordered to relieve Budapest.

Wiking forces during a defensive operation in Hungary in early 1945. Fighting around the Hungarian capital was fierce and unrelenting and Wiking and Totenkopf were forced onto the defensive. Soldiers of the Wiking division fought in atrocious conditions and were slowly bled to death by incessant Soviet attacks.

Panzergrenadiers being transported across the snow on board Sd.Kfz.251 halftracks in Hungary. In spite of Wiking and a number of other premier Waffen-SS divisions, notably Totenkopf, fighting fiercely to hold the front in Hungary, the Red Army smashed its way through the German defences and wrenched open a gap more than 60 miles wide. Within ten days of the Red Army opening its counter-offensive it had pushed its way through the Vertes mountains across three major rivers and had smashed to pieces the German formations opposing it. Although Wiking retreated into Czechoslovakia, exhausted and depleted units still remained to support the 6th SS Panzer Army as it withdrew.

A knocked-out Sd.Kfz.250 Ausf.B in a destroyed street with dead crew strewn around the vehicle. Note the division's insignia painted on the front of the halftrack. Wiking did what it could to protect withdrawing German Panzer and infantry forces as it fell back under a storm of Russian firepower. Remnants of the division withdrew to Vienna where they fought to the bitter end to defend the city. It was here outside the Austrian capital that the Wiking division, with its predominantly western European troops, was annihilated. A few escaped the slaughter and surrendered to American forces near Fürstenfeld on 9 May 1945.

Appendix

Order of Battle

Order of Battle (December 1940)

Stab
SS-Regiment Germania
SS-Regiment Nordland
SS-Regiment Westland
SS-Artillerie-Regiment 5
SS-Nachrichten-Abteilung 5
SS-Pionier-Bataillon 5
SS-Panzerjäger-Abteilung 5
SS-Aufklärungs-Abteilung 5
1 und 2 Sanitärs-Kompanie
1–3 Werkstatt-Kompanie

Order of Battle (26 May 1941)

Stab
SS-Infanterie-Regiment Germania
SS-Infanterie-Regiment Nordland
SS-Infanterie-Regiment Westland
SS-Artillerie-Regiment 5
SS-Artillerie-Meßbatterie
SS-Nachrichten-Abteilung 5
SS-Pionier-Bataillon 5
SS-Panzerjäger-Abteilung 5
SS-Aufklärungs-Abteilung 5
SS-Flak-MG-Bataillon
Nachschub-Dienst
Sanitäts-Dienst
Ordnungsdienst

SS-Panzergrenadier Regiment 9 Germania
SS-Panzergrenadier Regiment 10 Westland
SS-Panzer Regiment 5
SS-Panzer Artillerie Regiment 5
Finnisches Freiwilligen-Bataillon der Waffen-SS (until 1943)
Estnisches SS-Freiwilligen-Panzer-Grenadier-Bataillon Narwa (1943–44)
SS-Panzerjäger-Abteilung 5
SS-Sturmgeschütz-Abteilung 5
SS-Sturmgeschütz-Batterie 5
SS-Flak-Abteilung 5
SS-Werfer-Abteilung 5
SS-Panzer-Nachrichten-Abteilung 5
SS-Panzer-Aufklärungs-Abteilung 5
SS-Panzer-Pionier-Bataillon 5
SS-Dina 5
SS-Instandsetzungs-Abteilung 5
SS-Wirtschafts-Bataillon 5
SS-Sanitäts-Abteilung 5
SS-Feldlazarett 5
SS-Kriegsberichter-Zug 5
SS-Feldgendarmerie-Trupp 5
SS-Feldersatz-Bataillon 5

Notes

Notes

Notes

Notes

Notes

Notes

Notes

Notes